# Introduction

Mark Fidrych's funny antics on
the mound had baseball fans
laughing all during the
summer of 1976.
He talks to baseballs.
Between innings he gets down on
his hands and knees and pats
the dirt on the mound.
He cheers loudly for his
Detroit Tiger teammates.
But he is also a great pitcher
and has brought a new spirit
to the game of baseball.

# Mark "The Bird" Fidrych

## S. H. Burchard

Illustrated with photographs

Harcourt Brace Jovanovich
New York and London

For John Stifel

Frontispiece: Mark "The Bird" Fidrych of the Detroit Tigers
talks to the baseball.

Library of Congress Cataloging in Publication Data

Burchard, S    H
    Mark "The Bird" Fidrych.

    (Sports star)
    SUMMARY: An easy-to-read biography of the Detroit Tigers pitcher who
was named Rookie of the Year in the American League in 1976.
    1. Fidrych, Mark, 1954–    —Juvenile literature.   2. Baseball players—
United States—Biography—Juvenile literature.   [1. Fidrych, Mark,
1954–    2. Baseball players]  I. Title.
GV865.F426B87     796.357′.092′4 [B] [92] 77–4685
ISBN 0–15–278012–2
ISBN 0–15–684826–0 pbk.

# Contents

# 1

# The Boy Who Could Not Sit Still

Mark Steven Fidrych was born
  on August 14, 1954.
His father was Polish.
His mother was Danish.
Mark grew up in the pretty town
  of Northboro, Massachusetts.
Mr. Fidrych was a teacher and
  then became a principal in a
  junior high school.

Main Street in Northboro, Massachusetts

The Fidrych family grew until
　　there were four children.
Mark was the only boy, and it
　　was hard to keep track of him.
One day he was shopping with
　　his mother.
He got tired of waiting for her
　　and ran off to explore.
Mrs. Fidrych looked all over
　　the big shopping center for
　　her missing son.
She finally saw some people
　　standing in front of a
　　department-store window.
Three-year-old Mark was peeking
　　out from the other side of
　　the glass.

8

This is where Mark went to grade school.

He had drawn his first crowd.
When he went to school, Mark
   had to repeat the first and
   second grades.
It was hard for him to sit
   still and listen to the
   teacher and not wiggle or
   make strange noises.

# He would rather have been playing outdoors.

Mark often played baseball on this street
in front of his house.

Mr. Fidrych could see that his
active son was better at
sports than at schoolwork.
He taught Mark to bowl and to
play baseball.
Mark loved baseball.
At night he put his glove under
his mattress.
He wore his baseball cap to bed.
After he pulled up the covers,
he yanked his cap over his
eyes and went to sleep.

The Fidrych home in Northboro

# 2

# Mark Becomes a Pitcher

By the time Mark went to
Algonquin High School, he was
a fine athlete.
First-year students were not
allowed to play on the
varsity team.
So Mark became a member of the
freshman jayvee team.
With Mark pitching, the jayvee
team beat the varsity team.

Mark was good at everything.
He could hit well.
Sometimes he was an outfielder
   and sometimes a first baseman.
He also played basketball and
   football.

The Algonquin High School has
a big parking lot and many acres
of playing fields.

That summer Mark tried out for
the American Legion team.
The best players from all the
high schools in the area play
on Legion teams.
Mark told Coach Ted Rolfe that
he wanted to pitch.
After Coach Rolfe watched Mark
throw only one ball, he said,
"Here is a kid who really has
something."
Mark pitched his first Legion
game against a tough team
from Fitchburg, Massachusetts.
It was a no-hitter.
Mark struck out fourteen
batters.

Coach Rolfe did not have to
   teach Mark how to pitch.
Mark taught himself.
He spent many hours every day
   practicing.
He learned how to have almost
   perfect control over the ball.
He could place the ball just
   where he wanted it.
Usually he threw low, hard
   strikes.
One thing that great athletes
   must do is to keep their
   minds on what they are doing.
To keep his mind on the
   baseball, Mark began saying
   things to it.

16

Talking or just making sounds
helped him to concentrate.
Nobody seemed to think there
was anything odd about a
pitcher talking to the ball
and making strange noises.

American Legion coach Ted Rolfe

Mark got along well with his teammates.

His excitement for the game was catching.

All during a game Mark would yell to his teammates in the infield and outfield.

He cheered them for their good plays.

He comforted them when they made mistakes.

Everyone played better when Mark was on the mound.

Big crowds began to come to the games.

Some of the people were scouts from pro teams.

18

High school coach Jack Wallace

In three summers, Mark won
sixteen games and lost only
three for the Legion team.
His record on his high school
team was not as good.
Jack Wallace was a strict coach,
and some of the team did not
like following all of his rules.

Mark did what he was told,
putting a jacket over his
T-shirt on a very cold day and
even cutting his long, curly
hair.
It was very difficult for Mark
to walk anywhere.
He always wanted to run.
One time he was running down
the hall.
When his science teacher, Miss
O'Connell, came out of her
classroom loaded down with
books, Mark could not stop in
time.
Books went flying everywhere,

Both the high school and
the American Legion teams fought
their battles on this field.

and Mark and Miss O'Connell
    ended up on the floor.
As he helped Miss O'Connell to
    her feet and picked up the
    books, Mark said over and
    over, "I'm sorry. I'm sorry."
All day long he kept coming
    back to apologize.

Mark did not go back to
    Algonquin for his last year
    of high school.
At nineteen, he was too old to
    play on the baseball team.
So Mark's parents decided to
    send him to a private school
    near their home.
It was there that Joe Cusick, a
    Detroit Tigers' scout, came
    to see Mark.
The scout liked what he saw.
He wanted the Tigers to draft
    Mark.
After he finished high school,
    Mark worked in a gas station
    in Northboro.

22

The owner of the Pierce Gas Station
said Mark was always full of energy.

He earned two dollars an hour.
One day Mr. Fidrych came
   running into the station looking
   for his son.
"You don't have to work here
   anymore," he said, almost out
   of breath.

Curly-haired Mark sits on his front steps
with his dogs Domino and Lady.

"You got another job!
The Tigers want you."
Being asked to join a major
    league ball club was a dream
    come true.
On June 9, 1974, nineteen-year-
    old Mark Fidrych signed the
    paper that made him a pro
    ballplayer for the Detroit
    Tigers.

# 3

# Playing in the Minors

Mark soon left home to go to
   the beginning Tiger farm club
   in Bristol, Virginia.
On the first day of practice,
   Mark startled his teammates.
As the tall, skinny pitcher
   loped onto the field, he let
   out an ear-splitting squawk.
"Gaawk! Gaawk!" yelled Mark as
   he raced around the field.

Mark is an expert bubble blower.

"A bird. He's a bird!" said
   Coach Jeff Hogan, shaking his
   head in amazement.
The new name stuck.
Mark won three games and lost
   none at Bristol.
He played so well that he began
   the 1975 season playing for
   the Tigers Class C farm club
   in Lakeland, Florida.

Tigertown Baseball Stadium
in Lakeland, Florida

He lost a few games, but the
coaches were still impressed
with his concentration and
control of the ball.
In his spare time Mark earned
extra money by opening up a
car wash in the stadium parking
lot.

Mark set up his car-wash business
in this parking lot, which was often
filled with sea gulls.

Soon Mark was promoted again.
This time he went to
    Montgomery, Alabama, where
    he played for only one month.
His next move was to the
    Evansville, Indiana, triple A
    ball club.
It was his last stop before the
    major leagues.
There he quickly became one of
    the best minor league pitchers
    in the country.
He also became known for his
    enthusiasm.
After winning one important
    game, Mark ran to homeplate
    and gave his catcher a kiss.

Then he raced off to center
field, where he hugged and
kissed the fielder who caught
the last ball.
By the end of the summer of
1975, the stories of Mark's
funny antics—and his ability
—began to reach Detroit.

# 4

# "The Bird" Who Becomes a Tiger

The Tigers were in last place
in their league for the
second year in a row.
They had one of the worst
records in the major leagues.
They needed help in a big way,
and they sent for Mark.
Only two years out of high
school, Mark Fidrych had made
it to a major league team.

33

Mark in his major league uniform

His new teammates thought he
   was a little crazy, but they
   liked him.
He raced in and out of the
   dugout even in practice.
He almost never stopped talking
   or yelling.
He was so eager that it was fun
   playing with him.
But Mark got off to a slow
   start as a major league
   player.
He did not pitch very well in
   spring training.
The first five weeks of the
   1976 season Mark spent
   sitting in the dugout.

Mark sits in the dugout
and blows a half-hearted bubble.

Finally Manager Ralph Houk gave
him his big chance.
He was named the starting
pitcher on May 15 against the
Cleveland Indians.
On the day of the game, Mark
looked out of the window of
his small Detroit apartment
and saw that it was raining.
When he got to the ball park,
the parking lot was almost
empty.
Not many people came to watch
Mark pitch his first game.
But the drizzling rain and the
small crowd in the stands did
not bother Mark.

The new rookie tries to do his best.

He was too excited about his
   first start.
He tore out to the mound and
   went right to work.
For six innings he kept the
   Indians from getting a hit.
His teammates and the fans
   could not believe their eyes.
Mark held the ball up and
   talked to it.
"Get it over there now.
   Get it on!" he said.
He pointed and aimed and said
   a few more words to the ball.
Before each pitch he made fast
   circles with his arm like a
   windmill.

Mark carefully pats dirt over the holes
made by his cleats.

Mark did everything he could
think of to keep his mind on
the ball and get it over the
plate.
At the beginning of each inning
he got down on his hands and
knees to smooth out the dirt
around him.

He patted it carefully into
place.
Only three other major league
pitchers in the history of
baseball had no-hitters in
their first game.
Mark was on his way to being
the fourth when his no-hitter
came to an end in the seventh
inning.
Two Cleveland batters got hits,
and a run scored.
Mark did not let the loss of
his no-hitter get him down.
"O.K., so your no-hitter is
gone," he told himself and
the ball.

"You can still win the game."
He got the next eight Indians
   out without a hit.
The Tigers won by a score of
   2 to 1.
Very few new pitchers had ever
   done better.

# 5

## "Go, 'Bird,' Go!"

Mark's next start was against
    the Boston Red Sox.
Two busloads of friends and his
    parents came to watch.
Mark talked like crazy to the
    ball and pitched a good game.
But he got no help from the
    Detroit batters.
The Tigers lost by a score of
    2 to 0.

Mark Fidrych rests while he waits
for the next batter.

After Boston, Mark really began
   to fly.
He won six games in a row.
With each win, Detroit baseball
   fans got more and more
   excited.
Here, finally, was someone who
   could win baseball games.
They loved him even more
   because of the whacky things
   he did when he pitched.
They called him "The Bird," the
   name he had picked up in the
   minor leagues.
They also thought Mark looked
   like Big Bird on "Sesame
   Street."

44

"Big Bird" gives Mark a few batting tips.

He was tall and skinny and had
fluffy yellow curls.
His arms were floppy as he
moved.
He had big round eyes, and his
mouth was usually open.
He even had the quick
movements of a nervous bird.
When "The Bird" was pitching,
he flew out of the dugout as if
he could not wait to get
started.
"Go, 'Bird,' go!" screamed the
wild "Bird" fans.
After saying a few words to the
ball, Mark would bend over, go
into his quick helicopter

46

windup, and hurl the ball
toward homeplate.

"The Bird" in action

The best thing was that "The
    Bird" was not just funny.
He was a terrific pitcher.
He usually threw low, and he
    threw strikes.
He threw as hard at the end of
    a game as at the beginning.
Just about everybody in
    Michigan became a "Bird" fan.
Teen-age girls swooned over him.
Kids hounded him for his
    autograph.
Reporters never left him alone.
A member of the Michigan
    government tried to get the
    Tigers to raise Mark's
    $16,500 salary.

Mark signs autographs for his fans.

But Mark was working hard at
  being a super star.
He was having the time of his
  life.

# 6

# "The Bird" Meets the Yankees

By the time he faced the Yankees
at Tiger Stadium on Monday
night, June 28, Mark was
almost a national hero.
Close to 10,000 fans were
turned away because they
could not get tickets.
They had to go home and watch
the game on television along
with people in about nine

A close-up of the Tiger rookie

million other homes across
the country.

The fans who got into the
stadium almost never stopped
screaming for Mark.

"Go, 'Bird,' go!" they yelled
even during his warm-up
pitches.

Mark did not let them down.

When the game began, he ran out
to the mound.

He wiggled his knees and did a
few exercises.

The Yankees were one of the
strongest teams in baseball
and would be a tough team to
beat.

Mark talking to the ball

Mark almost never stopped
   talking to himself or to the ball.
The first batter grounded out.
Mark struck out the next two
   batters.
His teammates helped by getting
   two runs in the second half
   of the first inning.
The Yankee catcher, Elrod
   Hendricks, got a homerun in
   the second inning.
After that the game belonged to
   "The Bird."
No Yankee player got past
   second base for the rest of
   the game.

Mark takes careful aim.

The Tigers got three more runs
    and won by a score of 5 to 1.
The fans exploded with cheers.
Mark exploded, too.
He ran all over the field
    hugging teammates and
    groundskeepers, shaking hands,
    and even hugging himself.
Then he ran into the locker
    room for a television
    interview.
But the crowds would not leave.
They began to chant louder and
    louder, "We want 'The Bird!' "
They became so noisy that
    something had to be done.
Finally Mark went back out on

56

Mark comes back and says good night
to almost fifty thousand cheering fans.

the field, taking some of his
teammates with him.
Standing in his stocking feet,
    "The Bird" laughed and waved
    to his fans.
The crowd went wild.
Nobody had ever seen anything
    quite like it.

# 7

# A Bicentennial Hero

After the Yankee game on
　　national television, Mark was
　　the talk of baseball fans
　　everywhere.
By the middle of the season,
　　he had won thirteen games
　　and lost four for the Tigers.
He was named professional
　　athlete of the month for July.
Then came the biggest honor of
　　all.

Mark getting ready to fire the ball

He became the first rookie in
fifty years—only the
second in history—to be
named a starting pitcher in
the All-Star game.
But the bats of the powerful
All-Star Cincinnati Red
players were too much for
Mark.
The National League scored two
runs in the first inning.
Mark pitched one more inning
and then was taken out of the
game.
The American League lost by a
score of 7 to 1.

Mark winds up to pitch.

After the All-Star game, Mark
   went right on talking to the
   baseball and packing the
   stands with fans for the rest
   of the summer.
He was usually very good.
But he had some bad days, too.
The Tigers did not come close
   to winning the pennant, but
   they played better than they
   had for a long time.
Mark won nineteen games and
   lost nine.
After the season was over, he
   was named the American
   League's Rookie of the Year.
Some people may wonder why

Two of America's favorite birds

there was so much excitement
about a skinny, whacky twenty-
two-year-old rookie pitcher.
For one thing, he made people
laugh with his silly antics.

He played with an enthusiasm
people had not seen in a long
time.
He brought new spirit to
America's favorite game in
the Bicentennial year.
It is too soon to know whether
or not Mark Fidrych will be
an all-time great pitcher.
But he gave baseball fans a great
summer and a promise of more
to come.

64